POACHER'S PIE

Ted Ingle

Edward Ingle
india.inc

First published in Scotland in 2001
india.inc

Cover photographs property of Edward Ingle
Jacket design by mode

ISBN 0-954 1829-0-1

Printed in Scotland by Allander Litho, Edinburgh

THE BALLAD OF TED INGLE – SOMETHIN' FISHY

I wis drinkin' in the Mercat when I bumped intae this bloke,
An' his troosers looked as though pit in the tub tae soak,
An' he offered me the contents o' a muckle plastic poke,
An' I thought "There's somethin' fishy goin' on!"
What's in the bag, sir, what's in there?
It's strecht frae the Tyne an' it's dreepin' on the flair!
There's a policeman in the corner wi' a cauld suspicious stare,
For he kens there's somethin' fishy goin' on!

The prood Cockinny fishermen they plough the raging deep,
An' the anglers on the Whiteadder their weekend vigils keep –
But whae's that splashin' in the Tyne while hornies sleep?
Oh, I think there's somethin' fishy goin' on!
What's in the bag, sir, (etc)

Wi' a lump o' salmon on his plate a man can dine in styoe,
Or if ye want tae flog them ye can mak yersel a pile –
But the money's no much use when ye're sittin' in the jyle
When they ken there's somethin' fishy goin' on!
What's in the bag, sir, (etc)

I jan whit's in the grunie, gadgie, nash aff oot o' here,
For ye chored them for the pannie, noo we'll tober oot o' here,
For the stardie's deekin' at us, an it's time tae disappear –
For he kens there's somethin' fishy goin' on!
What's in the bag, sir, (etc)

David Robertson

"In thirty years of plundering
the countryside I have never
taken a fish, animal or bird
except for food or money."

Ted Ingle

INTRODUCTION

The stories you will find in this book are all firmly based on fact, although here and there I have taken a writer's licence and allowed my imagination to add some extra colour. Also, for various reasons, people and places have sometimes been changed.

It is not my intention to convert you to poaching ways, nor even persuade you to approve of them if you already do not. My intention is simply to entertain by recalling a few of my experiences, gathered over thirty years of plundering the countryside, causing havoc amongst the gentry and their hired help.

Most of my poaching expeditions were successful but now and then the long arm of the law reached out and I found myself in court, faced with the option of a fine or a prison sentence. Being a fresh air fanatic, I was never happy when an iron cell door was bolted behind me, so I usually paid the fine if I could afford it. Over the years I reckon I have parted with somewhere between nine and ten thousand pounds.

My methods of catching animals, birds and fish are as humane as I could possibly make them. Either they die within seconds or they escape unhurt. I have never used any kind of poison. On the very few occasions I have tried explosives – and that was many years ago – I caused more harm to myself than to the fish!

In short, even the landowners, bailiffs and police never tied me in with that other class of poacher whose disastrous and lunatic methods were, and still are, to riddle deer with bullets or throw a tin of poison into the water, take a few contaminated fish...and kill everything else in the river.

As for myself, I have never killed any animal, bird or fish except for food, or for money – offered to me by someone who didn't mind buying his food outside rather than inside the butcher's shop.

Ted Ingle
Haddington, East Lothian

EDWARD 'TED' INGLE

One of twelve children, Ted was born on 27th May 1941 (the day the Bismarck was sunk!) in Haddington, East Lothian. His father had been born and raised in Australia – where Ted's grandfather had been sent for sheep stealing – and had served in the 9th Division of the ANZAC at Gallipoli. Later, while serving with the KOSB in the Borders, he met Ted's mother and together they tramped the moors with a pram in 1926, the year of the General Strike. Having served in three wars ("counting the Irish one") his father eventually became RSM with the 4th Gurkhas.

Ted attended Knox Academy in Haddington, "but wasn't a very good scholar. I would sooner jump in the burn than go. I hated it all except for nature study." Leaving school at fifteen he became a woodcutter and fencer, while also rearing pheasants, before joining the army in 1958 as a regular soldier in The Black Watch, based at Queen's Barracks, Perth. Among his first duties was guarding the ospreys at their nesting site in Strathspey – and the Royal Family on holiday at Balmoral.

Though never ranked higher than Private – with a talent for "plundering compo rations, hard tack and tinned sweets!" – he was posted to Cyprus during the troubles and spent some time with the SAS as a sniper. On returning to this country in 1962, he spent time as a guard at Portendown before being demobbed in Germany, half a mile from Belsen, at the end of his six-year engagement with a demob credit of £11 12/-.

He married in Somerset, before seeking work in a power station and as a diver in Shetland.

> "My poaching skills are quite natural and instinctive, as they are among countrymen whose families have inhabited their countryside for centuries. My mother had a family connection with the Faas – the gypsy kings and queens of Yetholm." *Ted Ingle*

CONTENTS

JUST A NORMAL DAY

THE NIGHT WAS windy – not the best of times to be plundering salmon and sea trout, because if keepers are about it is hard to see or hear them in the dark. A still night is always best, as sound carries great distances and you can hear them coming long before they get close.

I had been down to the river earlier in the day and seen the fish jumping in one of the pools after the heavy rain. So now it was out with the foulhook to drag the bottom of the pool, hoping to make contact with any fish lying in its deadly path. I had already drawn out two fine sea trout that morning and knew there were others. As I lay in the shadow of an aspen tree, listening for any unusual noises, I ran up my rod with its heavy-duty reel – seven feet six inches of solid fibreglass with sixty-pound gut and a one inch treble hook with lead weight attached. This is a deadly combination in the right hands. You can take virtually any size of fish with this contraption in a few moments, no matter how fresh-run they are.

At the second cast of this fiendish device I hit into a fish. He was a five pounder, pure silver – a sea trout, leaping and thrashing. I pulled him quickly from the pool and hid him. Sometimes this sport is so fast – a fish with every cast – that there is no time even to hide them.

This night was no exception, for I had ten out in twenty minutes, totalling about forty pounds weight – quite enough to carry the five miles home.

Just as I was taking the hook off I either heard a sound or some sixth sense told me that others besides myself were afoot that windy night. Putting a stone into the tattie bag along with the fish I hastily tied the neck and dumped the lot back into the pool. Not a moment too soon, as I then saw the bailiffs climbing the dyke not twenty yards away. Rushing up to me (there were four of them) one shone a torch in my face.

“Where is the fish you caught, you bastard?” he screamed, illuminating the blood and scales on the ground nearby.

“I never got any,” I informed him humbly. “There was some other body doon here afore me.”

They raked up and down for a while but never found the bag. Picking up my gear, in which they had found only ordinary fishing flies and tackle, I made my way home.

I collected the fish the next day at the time when the keepers went for their dinner. That bunch did everything together – terrified of getting a hammering from the poachers!

A CASE FOR THE PF

ONE DAY I was painting a farm roof near where I was staying. Around the farm is a fairly big estate. While I was thus employed I beheld two of my sons coming down the track towards me. I looked more closely and saw they were leading something on a piece of string. I soon identified this as an old crow, more or less on its last legs.

"Where are you going with that?" I enquired.

"We found it up in the wood, faither," they replied. "It seems to be quite tame. It might make a good companion for the duck." (We had an Aylesbury duck which was, of course, pure white.)

Now, a few weeks before, the burgh happened to have acquired a new Procurator Fiscal. This important person had become very busy trying to make a name for himself by sending *me* a continuous stream of threatening letters concerning the fines he alleged I had failed to pay.

"Lads," I said, "I'll tell you what you can do with that old crow..." I suggested a course of action and off the boys went with the crow and their lurchers.

Two days later I came out of the local pub to observe a police car close at hand.

"Can we have a word with you, Ted?" asked the constable, quite politely.

"What's it about?" I replied, trying to conjure up ideas of what I might and might not have done in the course of the past week.

"It's about a crow," said the constable.

"A *crow*," I said, thinking first of one or two of the ladies in the bar I had just left. "I never touched them," I protested.

"Not that kind. We mean the kind that was inserted through the letterbox of the PF's office the other day."

He then related to me how, once inside the office, the bird had made a nest out of the summonses and charge sheets, after tearing them to bits, so that when the typists came in they found her placidly settling down in the 'Out' tray on a pile of torn paper.

Apparently the uproar in the ensuing minutes had been really something to be witnessed, as I learnt later from another constable who spoke to me in the street. For some reason he looked at me suspiciously.

It seemed that the police had been called, and they took the bird away in a box and handed it to a retired gamekeeper who made a hobby of keeping injured or disabled animals and birds.

Naturally I denied all responsibility or even knowledge of the affair, but then as the officer was walking away I couldn't resist calling after him, "Did the bird have a piece of binder twine on its leg, constable?"

He affirmed that it had.

"Ah well, I ken nothing at all about it," said I, walking off hastily before he came to his senses!

DAY OF THE LONG KNIVES

SANDY CAME INTO the bar just as I was about to finish my fourth pint.

"What have you been up to," he enquired.

"Nothing much," said I. "The weather's too nice. The keepers will be out in full force."

"I wouldn't mind coming out with you sometime," said Sandy, buying the next round of drinks.

"Well, okay," I replied. "But it might be a bit dangerous on account of your weak eyesight. And how will you comport yourself when it comes to fisticuffs?"

"Oh, I can handle that well enough," says Sandy. True, he's a big enough lad.

We blethered on and on, and after our sixth or eighth pint we decided to go and see what we could catch in the way of a sea trout or salmon. I duly got the net out of its hideyhole and sneaked – or should I say staggered – along the river bank. We soon came to a likely looking pool.

I said to Sandy, "Climb that tree and watch out for the bailiffs, while I run the net out."

With one person on the net (for the instruction of those who do not know much about such things) all you do is stick a branch of wood near the top of the pool, tie the net to it and swim over, playing the net behind you.

When you reach the far bank you should be at least fifteen yards further downstream. You then tether the net and swim back to take the other end and walk down till the net is stretched tight. Anyway, I had done half the pool by this time and the fish were starting to hit the net when I heard a noise. Upon looking up I saw two keepers prancing up and down like mad morris dancers on the opposite bank.

Sandy immediately made a bolt for it. I tried frantically to pull

the net back to my side, but two more of 'The Enemy' arrived there and I had no option but to beat a fast retreat myself.

Well, what with all the pints of beer and the wet clothes I had on, the second pair came close on my heels. They were a father and son, the son being the faster.

"Bugger this for a carry on," I told myself.

Strapped to my leg was a diver's knife with a stainless steel blade, ten inches long. This was for use if I got into any kind of trouble in the water, getting caught up in the nets or whatever.

The man and the boy stopped dead in their tracks.

"He's got a big knife, faither," says the son.

Now it was my turn to roar, sort of fumbling with the knife. I made straight for them. It seemed they suddenly lost their bottle, for they turned and bolted.

Still roaring, I staggered and tripped after them, but by this time they were off across the footbridge, with the son trying to pass his father.

I retreated to the safety of a barley field and watched them hassling Sandy, whom they had easily caught, until a police car arrived. I had been rolling about laughing – but smiles vanished when they set two police dogs across the bridge and onto my scent.

I crawled for another hundred yards through the lonely field. One dog was getting close so I had to make a run for it. Bent double, I raced for a small lade which runs out of the river at the weir. This is fairly deep, but in I jumped, reached the far side and ran like hell for the big wood.

The dog was about a hundred yards behind me when I had a stroke of luck. A young couple who had been concealed in the corn suddenly stood up in some alarm only ten yards from the dog which, at once, made for them and took the young lad firmly by the hand while the lassie continued to adjust her clothing.

Meanwhile the other dog, still searching for me, ran towards a clump of willows. Here he put up three youths with fishing rods who were also violating the privacy of these lonely parts. They sufficiently distracted the dog for me to make my way to the village. There, in the pub, I never enjoyed a pint so much.

Indeed, the enjoyment was such that once again one pint led to another as I related the story of my recent adventure to the local hinds (farm servants).

After a while one of them remarked, "There's somebody looking through the window at you, Ted."

Sure enough, the two windows of the hotel were festooned with police hats.

Now, the bar has a door leading to the toilet, and from there you can get into the lounge. I made a bolt for it just as the Law burst in. I rushed through the toilet and into the lounge and was actually behind them as they scanned the bar for me. I made good my escape.

Sooner or later, of course, they had to catch me and that was the following week in the town – but only after another chase which took us all through a variety of alleyways and private gardens.

A month later Sandy and I went up before the Sheriff, charged with poaching salmon on a *Sunday* (God knows why) and threatening a bailiff with a knife.

Sandy got fined £100 – he also had a broken arm.

Then the Sheriff (who knew me only too well, of course) turned on me.

"What were you going to do with the knife you were threatening the keeper with?"

I said, "I'm sorry, your Eminence" – I forgot what you call a judge – "but I don't know. I was unable to catch him."

This brought wild guffaws from the public benches, of course.

A serious case, said the Sheriff. "I fine you £200 for poaching and £50 for threatening the keeper.

It wasn't too bad as I went out again the next night and did well enough to obtain all the necessary funds...!

A WELL-TRAINED DOG

WE HAD BEEN out all day and just as it was getting dark I said to my sons – Andrew, Edward and Shaun – "It's time to decamp. The boys will be around any minute now." I meant the bailiffs, of course.

Well, we had not got our gear together two minutes and were beginning to walk up a ride in the wood when out jumps the keeper, dragging a large Alsatian on a lead.

"Stand still," he shouts, "or the beast will tear you to bits!"

We duly came to a halt, not through fear of the keeper or his dog, but because we had not seen the latter before and wanted to know just how good or bad the brute was. He must be very new to the estate or our spies would have informed us long ago.

I accordingly said to the keeper, "Aye, it looks to be a vicious beast. I think you've got us this time."

"Give us the bag of fish over here," he commanded.

We, of course, had no intention of doing anything of the sort – these fish had been particularly hard earned.

"Maybe the dog's not so vicious after all," I ventured, trying to distract his attention. At that, my lads split up to surround the pair of them. They all had cudgels and had dealt with dogs of this variety before.

The keeper began to turn nervously round and round as we advanced on him in a ring, quite slowly.

"Keep away," he shouted. "I'll let him go and I'll not be responsible for his actions!"

The dog suddenly seemed to us to be about twelve feet long, but as we advanced it tried to get behind the keeper, winding the lead around the man's legs. I noticed it was very thin.

I gestured to the others to stop and, taking a half-eaten pie out of my pocket I offered it to the dog which nearly pulled the keeper off his feet in order to get at it.

It demolished the pie in two bites and then sat down and began to wag its tail.

"I can see it's well trained," I remarked to the keeper who, for some reason, was boiling with rage. Meanwhile, one of my lads fed it another pie.

For a minute or two we just stood around, grinning like cats. Then we all walked off up the hill.

"Leave the fish!" yelled the keeper. "If you don't leave the fish I'm going to let it go!"

"Why don't you take him for a wee walk?" I called back...at which he did, indeed, slip the lead and let go of the dog.

It sat down, quite pleased with itself.

"Get up," roared the keeper. "Attack! Attack!"

The dog did get up but merely went over to a small tree and lifted up its leg. It then wandered about, sniffing at the ground.

Completely losing his cool, the keeper now ran towards it, swinging the lead. He probably intended to deal the dog an encouraging blow on the flanks but, instead, caught it painfully on the nose.

The poor beast let out a yowl and, far from going for us, grabbed his master by the seat of his breeks. As the keeper tried desperately to pacify his pet – he had the cheek to shout at us, "Get it off me! Help me!" – we went on our way, laughing so much we could hardly stand.

YOU MUST PAY YOUR FINE!

I HAD BEEN fined £250 for my usual capers – £50 for accidentally dropping a stick on an under-keeper's head (this had made him perform a combination of St Vitus's Dance and a cannibal's reel) and £200 for the five fish I'd taken. Note the importance of the fish as compared with the keeper's head. I had been given six weeks to pay – which of course I had no intention of doing.

After numerous letters from the Sheriff Clerk threatening me with jail, the police duly came to lock me up. Naturally I bolted out the back and was obliged to stay in the woods for the following week – from time to time going into town to phone the wife to tell her where I could meet her (she was constantly being followed.)

False trails laid by her and my sons, and various other members of our large family, kept me free for another month but, as the summer drew to a close I got word from her: "Ye'll need to come hame – we need wood for the fire and the hoose needs decorating and the tatties need dug." Etc, etc!

So I came to the decision that I would give myself up in a week's time, but not before I had a good bevvy, just to fortify myself for the experience.

The chosen night came, and I duly disguised myself in an old army wig (obtained by the wife from a charity shop) together with an old frock and coat and a pair of dark glasses and a white stick.

I planned to enter a bar and order a pint of beer, meanwhile fumbling about in an old purse. From this I would take out some buttons, nails and foreign coins, with the odd ten pence piece, and hand them all to the barman (never to a barmaid) and then begin to gibber about being mugged in a nearby close. I could, of course, only do this once in any given pub.

I performed successfully three times, and the free drink I got was unbelievable, but in the fourth pub my downfall came when I landed up standing next to an old enemy whom I had

not seen for years. I couldn't resist nudging him.

"Remember me?" I enquired politely.

Of course he did not, looking the way I did. So, full of beer, lager, vodka etc as I was, I gave him a straight punch to the chin, knocking him to the floor. At this the other customers gave me somewhat astonished looks, with the landlord getting on the phone right away.

I knew I had not a moment to lose and bolted through the door.

As the police station was only a few hundred yards away I actually saw them running out, so naturally I took to my heels, with them in hot pursuit. Turning off the main street and up the hill I very soon came to the gates of a local mental hospital. The police seemed to have gone elsewhere.

Pausing for breath I now recalled that I actually had on me a note of referral to this same hospital from my own doctor, following a bout of severe and unexplained headaches. I pulled it out and made for the front door.

Staggering up to the nurse on duty I handed her the note and informed her, "I'm no' feelin' weel."

She stared at me and agreed, as well she might.

"Ye'll need tae see the Hoose Doctor."

The doctor duly appeared and it was then I think I put on my best bit of acting.

"First," he enquired, "why are you dressed up like that?" He looked curiously at my get-up, still complete with the old grey wig and white stick. He also noticed I was wearing a wellington on one foot and a sandshoe on the other.

"I keep taking these turns, doctor," I told him respectfully. "I threw myself into the river yesterday." (This at least was true, although I failed to mention the salmon I was after.) "I have a feeling, doctor, that I'm always being chased by the police and because of that I've been living in a midden for three months, and the only friend I've got are two rats – fact, I've got one with me here, in my pocket. Its name's Hamish."

I put my hand in my pocket but, at this, the doctor became very agitated and said, "No! No!"

They asked me some more questions and I got the impression they were beginning to have some doubts about me. They went off and had a conversation and then the nurse came back and said I could have a bath and a meal with the other residents while the doctor decided what to do.

I had a welcome bath and then, wearing a worn but clean jacket and trousers they gave me, I went into the dining room.

There were about a dozen of them, men and women, some with drink problems but most of them just old, which was not their fault of course. I was amazed at how well we were treated. Nobody got annoyed or shouted at us. During the evening we sat about and chatted or walked around the wards or watched television or played games.

I was still waiting to be officially admitted but, while watching the nine o'clock news, two policemen arrived as if by magic.

One of them said, "That's my boy!"

They slipped on the handcuffs and carted me off to the cells in the High Street in Edinburgh. I appeared before the Sheriff next day and was ordered to be confined in an asylum of quite a different sort – not half so comfortable and sympathetic!

DOMESTIC PETS & OTHERWISE

Some memorable encounters with the wild

A FAMILY AFFAIR

OFTEN I HAVE lain so still that golden-crested wrens have actually rested on my arm. Kingfishers are very shy but they have perched quite close in a tree overlooking the river. The cock bird will dive down and catch a minnow, bring it back and proceed to knock the fish on a branch. Then he will throw it to his wife, who always swallows it head first.

One day I was being pursued by the water bailiffs, as usual. I jumped into the river near some debris left by the floods. Placing a large pile of mud and twigs on top of my head, I stood in five feet of water, as still as I could. 'The Boys' came racing by, not giving the pile of rubbish in the water a second glance.

Then, about a foot away from me, a water vole suddenly appeared out of its hole in the bank at a point about level with my nose. From there it stared at me, not at all sure what I was supposed to be. I made no movement whatever and, in a few minutes, the whole family was there, each with a stalk of sedge in its mouth, sitting up on tiny star-shaped feet. Watching them, I forgot all about the keepers and it was another hour before I cleaned myself up and made my way home.

ROOKS ON THE MARCH

IF YOU HAVE ever been caught in fog so dense that you can barely see in front of you, you'll appreciate this story.

On one such day we were setting off to check a few snares we had set for pheasants. The fog was so thick we could not use our bicycles and were obliged to walk the two miles to the place which was near to a large rookery.

As we made our way along the old cart track, we became aware of something in front of us, something black, moving in the same direction. We soon identified it as a rook – and it was not alone. There must have been about fifty of them, walking in single file, heading towards their rookery. They made no attempt to fly (which they could hardly do anyway because of the fog). They were obviously very nervous but they ignored us.

This was the first and last time I ever saw large birds *walking* home!

A DISTRESSED NIGHTWALKER

ONE NIGHT WE were sleeping peacefully in the tent in the middle of a wood when we were awakened by a metallic banging coming from about ten yards away.

"What can that be?" asked my wife, somewhat alarmed.

"Why don't you go and enquire?" I replied.

"I will *not*," she squeaked.

I went myself and, to my astonishment, found a hedgehog with its head jammed into an empty bean can. It was wandering about, bumping into stones and trees.

I detached the can and the beast went on its way quite happily!

THE REGIMENTAL BADGER

WHILE I WAS in the army, with the Black Watch, we were once on guard on Salisbury Plain. That night we saw a badger being savaged by an Alsatian. We rescued it but the dog had ripped it right along its back, to the bone. So, when I came off stag, I got my housewife out and, with a bit of difficulty, we stitched up the gash and put a dressing of salt and alum on it.

At the same time I was in charge of another regiment's horses, so I put the badger into the stables and it became very tame. The officers were very interested and they all came down to see it. We kept it for six or seven months. It had not been much more than a bundle of fur when we got it but what with the feeding, including rabbits which I caught for it, it grew to an enormous size. However, there were badgers on the hill not far away. One day he disappeared and I reckon he must have taken off with them.

A few days later the commanding officer came round and said, "What's happened to your badger, Ingle?"

I replied, "It must have gone back to its native habitat, sir."

He was quite put out and went away muttering something about how it would have made a fine mascot, but the regiment seemed not to be good enough for it – or something like that!

A VICIOUS CONGER

THE NASTIEST of all the creatures you come across in fresh water or salt is the conger eel. Down at the mouth of the River Tyne, near Tyninghame, there is a deep hole where they dumped a lot of concrete blocks used during the war as barricades against tanks. The crevices and caves formed by these make ideal hiding places for fish – and other things.

On this day I was feeling about for the salmon which are usually there. When you feel the head you put in the snare, which is attached to your wrist, and ease it over until it's just past the lateral fins, then give it a jerk. Now I felt the head, and since it didn't back off, which is the way of the ordinary European eel, I thought it must be a salmon. I slipped on the snare and gave it a jerk.

Normally the fish comes out but this one didn't. I then felt teeth sink into my hand. I pulled and heaved but couldn't dislodge the snare, which is very strong. I eventually braced my feet against the bastion and hauled the beast out by main force. It was a huge conger eel about six feet long and six inches in diameter.

It tried to grab me by the hand again but I flung it onto the bank. I pulled out my eleven inch knife and skewered the eel to the ground through the neck. I was then able to take the snare off.

I was treating my torn hand with mud to stop the bleeding when I turned round to see that the eel had shaken itself free of the knife and slithered off back to the river. There are a lot of stories of how hard it is to kill an eel...and that is one of them.

THE UNDERWATER BUILDER

ANOTHER EXPERIENCE with an eel concerned a lamprey – the biggest I ever saw. It was about eight feet long, coloured brown and green like the camouflage on a wartime bomber. At first I thought it was a shark and then perhaps a Moray eel of the kind you get in deep sea waters.

I watched him for a while and he was doing a curious thing. He was using his huge sucker disc to collect stones and build them up into a heap. He was very very fussy where he put them, placing them in such a way as they wouldn't fall down, so building up a kind of pyramid.

The last one disturbed the surface of the water which was when I waded down and put a snare round him and hauled him well up the bank, just to admire the beautiful colouring. Some fish then appeared so I went back into the river and caught several. When I emerged for the last time the lamprey had vanished, having found his own way back to his native habitat.

A BONNY BIRD

A BIT LATER ON I kept quite a few animals at home. Among the first was a female sparrowhawk – that was about 1950. It had flown into telephone wires and broken a wing. Because my mother was related to the Faas of Yetholm there were still quite a few gypsies coming regularly to the house and it was they who showed me what to do.

The broken wing bone was actually showing. One of them took an ordinary stainless steel needle and pushed it into the bone on either side of the break – birds' wings are hollow, you see. He then squeezed the two ends together, taped it with thread and tied the wing to the bird's side.

We kept it that way for three weeks, not letting her move around too much. The wound didn't go sceptic and the bone knitted. In another week she managed to fly. We left the needle in.

We were staying on a farm then and the farmer used to bring his Clydesdale horse in at dinner time and leave it in the garden. We all used to jump on its back for the ride back to the steading, with our sparrowhawk sitting on the hames (the curved bars of the horse-collar). It was quite an unusual sight.

She was really part of the family for two years, then one day she took a fancy to the young chicks in the nearby steading and the farmer caught her at it.

He shot her – and that was the end of a really bonny bird.

FOXY FRIEND

FOXES MAKE great pets but the only one I ever kept I found by chance in a ditch. She was very small – a piner, as we call them – and she'd been shot. She was riddled with pellets but they'd only got under the skin, not quite far enough to disable her properly. So I took her home and we picked out the pellets which took some time.

She wouldn't eat so we used a baby's bottle filled with milk and a little caster oil and more or less forced the stuff down her throat.

In a few days she was eating normally and one day I went to pick her up and she bit me through the thumb, which showed she was certainly getting better. She used to follow us about like a wee dog but once she got bigger she just took her own way and we were quite happy to let her go, knowing she could look after herself.

BOBBY

ONCE WHEN I was netting a pool at the estuary of the Tyne I came on an otter which had been caught in a monocle net – the kind they hang in the sea – and it had escaped with a bad gash. I found her for the reason that the fish were behaving strangely. Something had disturbed them – they were racing round the pool, impossible to catch. So I came out of the water and then I heard whimpering.

I traced this to a shelf of rock and there was this beast just lying there, nearly dead from drowning and exhaustion. At first I couldn't get close to her because she was going to bite, but I went off and got a small brown trout and offered it to her. She took it in her hands and started to eat it, head first. Finally I coaxed her out and picked her up. She wouldn't have been very big. The net had cut deeply into her neck and chest and she'd made it worse by thrashing about. Sooner or later she'd have died.

So I took her home and worked away on her, using ordinary fishing gut and a needle and a drop of antisceptic liquid and installed her in the bath. In a few days she was running about – fighting with the cats – and when the wounds had finally knitted we took her to the river and actually used her in the catching of fish. We ran the net across and then threw her into the bottom of the pool, and then she drove all the fish into the net.

We kept her for about a year and a half, and then she too made her way back to where she came from. That was a long time ago now. I seem to remember we called her Bobby.

DEATH OF A HERON

IN THE COURSE of my pursuits I have become quite accustomed to seeing nature at its most gentle and its most violent.

Once, while watching the river for signs of 'The Enemy' – bailiffs or the police – I observed a heron peering into a pool about thirty yards away. Suddenly it made a downward swoop with its beak and withdrew from the water a large eel close to three feet long.

The heron somehow managed to get it by the head, and after shaking it about for while tried to swallow it. It succeeded in getting the head down its throat but the eel, far from defeated, wrapped the rest of its body two or three times round the bird's neck. Its head was still down the heron's throat and the bird could not or would not regurgitate.

As the life and death battle continued, the eel's weight became too much and the heron's head started to droop. Slowly it sank until it became completely immersed in the rocky pool. The eel never relaxed for a moment.

By the time I was able to intervene, the heron was dead – either drowned or strangled. The eel had managed to extricate itself and had swum away.

A RAT'S FLITTING

I WAS OUT ONE night with one of my boys, knocking pheasants out of the trees with a .410. At the end of the wood was a large midden built up with rubbish from the farm and the nearby cottages. Approaching this we became aware of a strange, loud squealing and rustling, as if caused by hundreds of small animals.

"Listen to that," I said to Andrew. "It's like the beardies are out in force."

Rats, as soon as they hear you, usually bolt for their holes, but not this time. I switched on my torch and there they were – hundreds of them, forming a grey mass which made the midden look as though it was alive itself. Even in the light of the torch they showed no sign of running away. Instead they turned as one and began to come towards us.

"Let's get out of here," I said. "They're after us!"

We turned and bolted and after three hundred yards stopped to get our breath. However, after two minutes we heard the rustling and squealing again, coming closer.

"Get up that tree," I told Andrew.

We scurried up the tree and sat there, awaiting the outcome. It did not take long. The screaming, gyrating mass surged towards us and then raced past below us in the moonlight.

We sat there for a full ten minutes, until all was quiet again.

"That is what's called a Rat's Flitting," I said. "Most people never see one, and if you do it's only once in a lifetime. And when it happens, make very sure you don't get in the way."

A VERY BIG CAT

A FEW YEARS ago one of the estate workers was down near the bank of the Tyne, near Dunbar, using a power saw to cut up an old dead beech. He suddenly became aware of a low growling, coming nearer, not at all like that of a dog. He couldn't actually see anything and he couldn't imagine what it was, so he took off at speed.

He told the story to a few people and then a couple of days later some animal made off with all his guinea fowl – and it wasn't a fox.

A few days after that I was coming up from the river near the same place, carrying three salmon. I had hit one of them a bit too hard and there was some blood about on the bank and the smell of it blowing on the wind. It was dusk, with a little snow on the ground, and I was walking up the ride carrying the fish to where I had parked the car in a sunken road.

After a hundred yards I sensed I was being followed. I saw a shape but couldn't identify it. It was just a shadow moving in and out of the trees. I still had four hundred yards to go and I knew it was coming closer. I made a run for it and plunged into the car. Then I realised that I had left the keys under the front wheel, so I had to get out and grab them. As I sat there, staring at the engine, I turned to see a pair of eyes staring through the gap in the dyke. They were enormous eyes – they must have been about five inches apart. I drove off.

Next day I went back to the same spot and, sure enough, there were pug marks of three-inch diameter on the soft ground. From the way the pugs had sunk in – indicating the pressure put on them – I reckoned the big cat must have weighed seventy or eighty pounds.

From later information we became sure that the beast was a puma, recently escaped from a wildlife park some twenty miles away!

SOME HINTS ON HOW TO CATCH FISH

IF YOU ARE out and about down by the river and see a salmon or a sea trout and unfortunately have nothing with which to catch it, consider the following advice.

First of all, never approach any fish from the front – always from the rear. Fish have the sharpest eyes in the whole of nature – they can even see you through murky water when the burn is in spate or coloured by peat. However, I have taken a fish out of the water when I have not been able to see it – although it has certainly been able to see me. Try and work that out!

Once, many years ago on a hot and brilliant July afternoon, I was walking up the river while the water was in spate – very yellowy brown it was. I had stopped to watch a pair of dragonflies dancing on the surface when I noticed also some bubbles erupting about two yards out from the bank.

At this point the river is normally two feet deep but because of the spate the depth had increased by more than a foot. I knew that at that point the river bottom was sandy, although then it was impossible to see more than two inches below the surface.

Anyway, I thought it strange the way the bubbles were coming up – but then, of course, there are twigs, branches or leaves producing a gas which rises in the form of bubbles every now and then.

As it happened, I had in my pocket what is known as a handline. This is ten yards of strong twine or cordline with a large treble hook attached to the end and, exactly two inches beyond that, a two ounce piece of lead.

The bubbles had lasted only a few seconds but, being of a curious nature, I felt compelled to find out what was causing them. Taking the foulhook out, I proceeded to swing the lead back and forward, letting it go well in front of the bubbles, knowing the current would take it down at least another foot. I then began to drag the line as close as possible to the place from where the bubbles rose.

On the near end of the line I had attached a small piece of elmwood five inches long, to wrap the line round as I drew it in. (Also to get a good and solid tug you need either a piece of wood or, failing that, the handle of your knife will do instead.)

Taking in as much slack as I dared, I gave the line a sudden heave. What happened next was unbelievable. An enormous salmon leapt out of the water and fell back in again, securely held by the hook.

Not entirely expecting this I stumbled and into the river I fell – still clutching the line, of course. The fish shot to and fro at a terrific pace, pulling me along with it. With the aid of a convenient branch I managed to haul myself up the overhanging bank, keeping a tight hold on the piece of elm attached to the tackle.

Soaking wet and somewhat shaken, I managed to retrieve the fish – it was more like a living person than a salmon. I stuffed it down the front of my camouflage smock and made for the nearest cover. When I got it home it weighed out at thirty nine and a half pounds – to my knowledge the biggest salmon ever taken from the River Tyne.

Thinking back on this incident, my guess is that the fish had either seen me or heard my footsteps and had instinctively expelled air from its air sac to give it more depth. I have seen this done many times while catching other fish by the same method.

Another poaching device is the staff-and-snare, as the Sheriffs call it. It consists of a willow wand as thick as your middle finger, about three feet long, and a snare made of brass wire. Six strands of wire are usually enough to pull out a good fish of up to ten pounds but over that you need more. If you make the snares yourself, a brass eyelet from an old boot is the thing to keep the snare running freely.

Once again, don't go for the fish from in front of him, if you can help it. As soon as you touch his nose he will be off or, if you do manage to get the noose over his head, once out of twice you'll lose him when he begins to thrash about. Worse still, if he succeeds in getting away, the damage probably done to his gills will eventually kill him. Naturally I don't favour that at all.

To return to the river. When you see your salmon or trout lying close to the bottom, make sure you do not cast your shadow over his or he will immediately decamp. Approach from behind, slide the snare under him and over his anal fin. When it surrounds the thinnest part of his waist, pull your staff towards you as hard as you can.

This will cause the fish to open his gills and will have the effect of stunning him for about three seconds – time enough for you to get a firm grip on your staff. Now drag him straight out of the water. On no account lower the stick, or that's the last you'll see of your catch – and don't try to kill him in the water either. Take him on to dry land and hit him (not too hard) between the eyes. If you hit him *very* hard the eyes will stick out of the head and that does not look very attractive on a fishmonger's slab.

My favourite equipment really is the net which comes in many forms – splash, strangle, gut, nylon, silk, cordline, trammel and many other variations. All can, of course, be used by a complete novice – provided he or she does not try to pull the thing *up* river!

I personally liked to use a nylon net with a three and a half inch mesh for sea trout, and four and a half inch for salmon. Remember that different rivers call for different ways of going about the business.

Once I took sixty-four salmon out of a river in Sutherland

with a bit of net ten yards long by nine feet deep. Altogether the salmon weighed nearly eight hundredweight! As we had only a shooting brake full of tenting gear (we often went up that way, presenting ourselves as a family of campers) we had to chuck out gas bottles, spare tyres, pots and pans, deckchairs – anything replaceable – in order to make room for this amazing amount of fish, which averaged fourteen pounds each!

AN INSPECTOR FALLS

ME AND MY YOUNG brother had gone down to the river towards 10pm. It had been raining during the past twenty-four hours and we were expecting a good run of sea trout. Knowing that the bailiffs would be out and about, we had to take care.

I had a seven-foot rod fitted with a Penn multiplying reel and line with a breaking strain of thirty pounds. My brother had a nine-foot rod and an ordinary fly reel with a twenty-pound line. The bait was our usual three-quarter inch treble hook and ball of lead rigged at the base of it. This method of fishing is known as snagging, or foulhooking, of course.

The technique is to cast the hook over to the opposite side of the pool and then reel in about two feet at a time. If you think you may be near a fish, you give it a yank. Either you hook a fish – or find it's a stone. The best time of day is late in the afternoon or evening, as dusk is falling.

In broad daylight, sea-angling gear is sometimes used. This, of course, is much heavier – but while using gut with a breaking strain of sixty pounds and feeling very confident, I have still had it broken by a fish of ten pounds or so. When a fish is 'on' – even only a seven-pounder – it will fight like mad, and many have I lost.

Anyway, this day we crept down to the pool and even before we got there we could hear the sea trout throwing themselves up the weir. In the course of our short walk from the main road we had rigged up our rods, so that all we had to do was take station and begin our fishing – although I suppose some would not call it that.

At the third cast I got into a three-pounder and had him out in no time. My brother hooked a fish as well. His being the more pliable rod, he had to ply his catch, which took longer.

However, we caught eleven fish in this way in fifteen minutes, carefully hiding each one some distance upstream.

(Never leave anything lying about the place when you are actually fishing).

I had just changed my hook, which had been bent by the knocks it had received, when I suddenly saw a light about twenty yards away. It was only a quick glimpse but I knew it must be a keeper with a cigarette in his hand. I waded down to my brother and said: "The Boys are behind us. When I tell you, get over the water as fast as you can."

A moment later we were up to our waists. Then all the torches went on. There were shouts and whistles but they did not feel inclined to swim across after us. We made our way upstream, collected the fish, re-crossed the river and made to bypass the scene of activity at the weir. Sure enough, there were the silhouettes of the keepers and the police against the neighbouring town lights. They were searching the banks for any fish or gear we had left.

I heard the well-known voice of a local inspector: "We'll get them if we have to turn out every night!"

For a time we lay and watched them, hidden by the darkness on the opposite side of the river. They showed no sign of moving off. The inspector was standing there, a perfect target, only thirty yards across the water.

It then occurred to me that we were lying in a potato field. We accordingly started to dig up tatties – they were Redskins, a very sound and thick-coated potato. We began to lob them into the crowd across the river. It was quite a spectacle. They couldn't see the missiles coming – they only heard the hum as they flew past their ears.

The inspector had been standing on top of the weir, watching the fish by the light of his torch. He never saw the big tattie that hit him on the side of the head, knocking him off balance into the pool below. The big splash, followed by shouts and yells, told us everything, and the confusion which reigned while his colleagues were pulling him out enabled us to make good our escape.

The next day I was back down by the river and met one of the local hinds (farm workers).

"Things are getting terrible dangerous about here," says he. "Somebody hit the inspector on the head last night with a big stone and all his nose is bruised from falling down the weir."

"Oh, is that so?" I naturally had to inform him, "I wouldn't know anything at all about *that*."

A SUMMER HOLIDAY

ABOUT JUNE WE used to depart from the house and camp out for a month or so. The aim was to have a working holiday – that is, poach all night and sleep now and again during the day.

On such occasions the first task is setting up and camouflaging the camp, getting the snares and nets ready and choosing positions from which to watch for the keepers – for if we are camping on an actual estate we have to be careful, and anyway all the kids are with us.

The second night we usually go down and net the river. Whatever fish we get we hide until the following morning, and then telephone our contact. He comes and collects – and pays us on the spot.

This particular year we decided to poach the eastern Highlands. We decamped in a hired motor caravan – me and the kids, my wife, Philip and my son Shaun and his girlfriend.

First we made for Braemar to see what the fishing was like there, but I saw only one fish of about ten pounds at the Lynn of Dee, so we moved on to the River Spey.

At Aviemore we camped beside the river. While the tents were being put up by the boys, I went to reconnoitre up river and found it to be most promising. The salmon were jumping like fleas and there was not a soul in sight.

We had our dinner and laid our plans – but the best-laid plans gang aft agley, and this time they did go agley with disastrous and hideous results...

Philip and I decided to net the big pool at once. Off we set, leaving the girls and kids in the big tent.

We netted the pool three times and got twenty-one salmon and eight large brown trout of about five pounds. The salmon were all around nine pounds, so with this huge weight we stumbled and peched back to the camp where we hid the fish in the river, close by.

Next morning I took some of the salmon to a hotel in Aviemore, and Philip went with a few more to the pub which was only two hundred yards from where we were camping.

He met a man in the bar and got talking and they had a good few drinks but, unfortunately, the man turned out to be an off-duty policeman. By the time I got back from the hotel they'd all got arrested and were in Aviemore which I had just left.

It seemed that Philip had returned to camp to fetch the three salmon the chap said he wanted and, when he returned with them to the pub, it was full of policemen. I had no choice but to go to Aviemore where they promptly locked me up too.

As there was so many of us, and the police weren't sure yet what we'd done, they put Philip and Shaun in the only two cells and told us: "You lot will need to stay in the caravan until we find out what's what."

I informed the inspector that it was impossible for us all to sleep in the caravan, for space reasons. He then agreed we should get the big tent and put it up on the lawn outside the police station, which we did. We stayed for five days!

Meanwhile the police had not touched any of my gear – nets and wetsuit – but had taken the rifle hidden under the seat of the van. This had a silencer and telescopic sights – excellent for roe deer. The CID came and questioned us as to its ownership, which nobody could recall...

By this time our money was getting short and the police agreed to let me go into the village to buy food. So I said to my wife (this was Thursday evening): "We'll need to get some cash. Away up to the caravan and put the net and the wetsuit into a bag. I'll tell the sergeant it's washing."

She did so. The sergeant looked at the bag but did not open it. Off we went as though making for the village but instead we cut down a pend and across a field to the river. There was a good pool here but there was also a footbridge not far away, with someone crossing now and again. However, it was dusk.

I told the girl to get her clothes off while I put on the wetsuit. So, dressed only in her underwear and enquiring nervously whether there were any eels, she got into the water with the end of the net and waded across the pool. We caught five fish, hid the net and the suit, sold the fish to the hotel, did our shopping and had a few pints.

When we got back to the police station the sergeant, who had been obliged to entertain the kids with a game of chess (which he had lost) enquired why we had been so long. I told him the truth by admitting we had looked into the pub for a drink. He was quite indignant and complained about having had to mind the bairns – and also accused them of cheating.

I suggested that since they were in his custody, it was his duty to look after them.

The following night we went through exactly the same routine, except that this time when we got back we found the inspector waiting for us. (We had netted ten fish but could only sell eight, and had hidden the two others with the net and suit.)

"I know what you're up to," said the inspector. "Look," he said, pointing to his ear, "it's not heather that's growing out of there." As we were half-gassed we had a closer look but his point, as it transpired, was that he and the sergeant were going fishing in the morning and that he needed a little help from me.

"I wonder," he asked, "if there could be any salmon in the pool at the footbridge? I have a bet with the sergeant that I'll get a fish before he does. We've fished that pool every Saturday for the past month and have failed to catch anything at all."

I thought for a bit and then said, "Well, Inspector, if you happen to look under the dead tree you'll maybe find a fish or two!" I knew full well what the rascal was up to.

Sure enough, on Saturday evening he and the sergeant came back from their angling highly delighted. The sergeant

had the eleven-pounder and the inspector the eighteen-pounder. The latter was especially chuffed and informed me confidentially, after a dram, that he had told the sergeant he caught both fish within fifteen minutes. (The sergeant had gone off to another pool.) But I don't think the sergeant really believed him because he accused me later: "I think the inspector and you is up to something!" Then he started to laugh.

On the Sunday they got rid of us. "Pack your kit and get away down the road," we were requested.

We hastily packed, managed to collect the suit and the net, and were given a police escort out of the village to make sure we really left. As they stopped to let us by they gave us a big wave, and we all waved back.

"A grand bunch of lads," we told each other.

***Postscript*:** *We had to leave poor Philip and Shaun locked up in the cells. On Monday morning they were fined £50 and £30 respectively. You can't win all the time!*

A BRUSH WITH THE KEEPERS

JOCK SAID TO ME one June day, "Do ye fancy a wee bap (walk)?" So off we set, making for a certain burn where we knew we could guddle a few trout in peace.

At the end of a wood and on the edge of a wheat field which was still green I caught the sound of voices.

"Hear anything?" I whispered to Jock.

"Aye," says he. "There's someone in the ditch dead ahead."

Creeping forward among the trees we espied two keepers on their hands and knees, peering up a cundy (field drain).

"They're poisoning a fox," said Jock. And sure enough, the swine were in the very act of pouring poison on to a spoon tied to a stick. We watched as they put in the poison and blocked the entrance with an old door and jammed it with a stob.

"We can clear it later," we heard the old keeper say, and they both went off towards the home farm for their dinner.

We gave them a little time and then slid through the green wheat and into the ditch, and crawled along to where they had been working. We removed the door and allowed a few minutes for the gas to clear.

Then Jock got out his matches, struck one and looked inside. There, five feet up the drain, was indeed a sorry sight. A vixen and her five cubs lay there, overcome by the gas.

"They've killed them all," I said.

"Dirty bastards," said Jock.

"Come on," says I. "The Boys will be back soon but if we're quick we can outwit them."

Getting a stick, I tied a snare on the end. Slipping it over the vixen's teeth, we pulled her out. Jock took his knife and cut the tail off, and we did the same with the rest of the litter.

(Keepers get a bonus for each fox's tail they can produce.)

"Right," says I. "Stuff them back up the cundy before the Boys come back."

Leaving everything as we found it we scrambled off to our own lair amongst the trees to watch the outcome.

It was not long before the keepers returned and proceeded to open up the cundy and pull out the foxes with a garden rake. Suddenly the expressions on their faces were a joy to behold.

"They've nae tails!" shouted the young keeper in blank amazement.

The old man gave a howl of rage. "Some bastard's cut the tails off ma foxes!" he yelled.

They proceeded to make a search of the area but never noticed Jock and me rolling about the wheat field in hysterics.

A NIGHT ON THE LOCH

IT ALL STARTED as a laugh, since it was the end of the kids' holidays and my wife uttered the usual suggestion: "Let's all get off to the Highlands for a week's camping."

After my last caper on the Braes of Mar I was not inclined to be over enthusiastic but finally she and the bairns won me over. Getting an old car was no problem, so off we set in the direction of the Western Isles – tent, nets, rods, hooks, wetsuit and all the paraphernalia that goes with an outing of this sort.

We stopped at Fort William but did not loiter as there were too many police for my liking. So on we went to Arisaig, Mallaig and the White Sands of Morar, where we camped in a field. (The old bastard of a farmer had the effrontery to charge us £2 a night – talk about Highland hospitality!) All he provided was a tap and a toilet, and all he did was moan at the bairns: "Do not be throwing stones at the cows," and "Stop chasing my ewes," etc etc.

After a few days the money started to run out on account of our having drunk most of it in the local hotel.

As we were leaving, the farmer said to us, "And what are you thinking of my camp site?"

"Well," I informed him, "I have been in camp sites all over the country and the only one I heard of that was better than yours was the one my father was at in France."

"Oh? And where would that be?" he intoned, quite chuffed.

"On the Somme in 1918," said I, and into the car we got hastily and drove back the way we had come.

At last we came to a remote loch with a small church standing beside it, and stopped to gaze at the water through field glasses.

About half a mile out I could see grilse throwing their fine silver bodies out of the water.

"Look at that," I said to the wife. "Two or three of those will solve our money problems." (By this time we only had £3 left, and the bairns were getting hungry.) "We'll wait until dark and then try for a few fish."

At that she laughed and told me, "That's a sea loch, not the River Tyne at Haddington. It's about nine hundred feet deep and you'll only drown yourself, you stupid old bugger."

"Don't worry, hen," I assured her politely. "If there's a fish in there I'll take them out."

I got the spare tyre from the boot, extracted the tube and proceeded to sew a tattie bag around it with twine, to make a floating container for the net.

By this time it was almost dark so I climbed into my wetsuit, tied a twenty yard piece of thin rope round my waist and attached the other end to the tube. The wind was getting up.

I instructed my wife, "Take the night glasses and keep an eye on me in case I get into difficulties." (I don't know what help she could have been but never mind.)

I waded in and swam slowly out, knowing full well that if I got into trouble I would never be seen or heard of again. I swam for a long time, towing the net in its floating sack. As my hands moved they disturbed phosphorescent creatures in the water which gave off a strange glow in the darkness.

By this time I had lost all fear and resigned myself to whatever lay in store. Suddenly there appeared alongside me two small orange lights, like torch bulbs, which then vanished and reappeared ahead of me, behind me and on the other side. Then I received a hard bang in the ribs, which gave me a fright but made me realise that this was only a friendly seal. It barked, and I replied with a loud shout, and it went on its way.

It was now time to lay the net. All I had to do was tie one end onto the tube and let the tide cause the net to slowly unfurl itself. It was only half way out when the salmon started to hit it. I held on to the near end of the rope with my teeth, backpeddling slowly towards the shore.

The net was ten feet deep and a hundred yards long, so that dragging it and the catch took a lot of effort. I eventually landed at the same spot, having allowed for the movement of the tide and the wind. Securing the net to a stone, I scrambled up to the car, which was in a lay-by, to find them all huddled down in their sleeping bags. So much for watching after my safety!

After banging on the window for about five minutes, I caused them to show face.

"Where have you been?" my wife squeaked. "We've been frightened to death."

"Frightened to death?!"

"There's something over there." She pointed to the large county council refuse bucket which was full of rubbish and had the usual mess round about it.

I went over and gave it a hearty kicking, and out rushed a huge rat. I returned to the car.

"Come on," I said impatiently. "Let's get these bloody fish out of the bloody net!"

This took us some time, as there were no fewer than sixty-nine salmon and sea trout in it and, once again, we had to throw away some of our gear in order to load them all into our vehicle.

Later that morning we sold half a dozen at a camp site which paid us enough for food and petrol, and the rest in Edinburgh for quite a princely sum. However, the thought remaining with me from that caper was that there was I, halfway out in a loch nine hundred feet deep, in fear of my very life, while my wife and family were cowering in the safety of a car, scared to death of a scabby Highland rat!

THE BEES

"DO YOU FANCY a turn with the sanre?" asked Shaun, my second oldest son.

"Well, we could," I said. "I saw some nice sea trout in the pool by the old willow tree – where the wild mink bit me on the knee."

(This young mink had seen me standing in the river from its place among the willow roots. It was only about eight inches long – just away from its mother – and it swam underwater and tried to make a meal of my leg. This attack tore my trousers but did me no harm.)

We took seven good sea trout from the pool – averaging nearly eight pounds. As we were walking – or should I say creeping – away, who should appear but the bold old keeper, shouting and bawling as was his wont in such circumstances.

He proceeded to chase after us. We decided that retreat was the better part of valour, so away we bolted towards the nearby farm buildings. These were disused except as a shelter for some machinery – and a number of beehives.

"Make for the hives, lad," I shouted. Shaun was a little ahead, as I was carrying the bag of fish.

We came to the hives and saw that the bees were fairly coming to and fro, it being a lovely day. As I passed one of the hives I gave it several sharp kicks.

"Keep on running," I yelled at Shaun, for indeed the bailiff was hard on our heels – but not for long. We heard roars and curses and turned to see the keeper enveloped in a huge swarm of furious bees which he was trying to beat off by waving his hat in the air.

We watched mesmerised as he gave up the battle and rushed back to the river, where he threw himself in, still beating himself about the head with his deerstalker hat.

We were indeed sorry to learn that he had reported himself

to the local hospital and, after treatment for a few stings, was advised to avoid interfering with beehives in the future.

What he said in reply is not on record!

A HIGH STEPPER

IT WAS A NIGHT in September when I decided to depart down the river to see if any fish had moved into the estuary following the heavy rain of the past few days. The snag was that I had been having a bit of trouble with the keeper on that estate and only the day before had narrowly escaped his clutches.

There was a half moon and a dim light as I cycled to my destination to hide my bike in a strip of wood, get my fishing rod tackled up and make my way to the deep pool where I was out to foulhook a few sea trout or salmon. After dark on such nights the fish usually congregated there in great numbers so that a treble hook with a lead weight, skilfully thrown in, was an easy method of making money.

As I crept down the side of the dyke I became aware of a strange silence. Normally there were a few birds roosting or fluttering in the trees, a couple of noisy hoody crows, some wood pigeons and a water hen or two – but tonight there was nothing. Some intruder must have disturbed them, so I was instantly on my guard.

A few moments later I caught the whiff of tobacco smoke and knew I was correct in my assumption. I had, of course, approached quite silently, and now I raised myself and peered very gingerly over the dyke.

Sure enough, there sat a keeper, huddled against the wall only about ten yards away. By his side was a .22 rifle and a game bag.

I froze, and stayed frozen for more than a minute, gathering my wits. Then I had an idea. I bent down slowly and pushed my hand into a puddle of water, holding it there for about thirty seconds. I inched forward until I was directly behind him, rose and placed my hand on the back of his neck, at the same time letting out a horrible cry.

The effect on the poor unsuspecting man was somewhat

astounding. He leapt to his feet and, with arms thrashing about, let out a sort of gibbering shriek. He then made off at great speed down through the field, jumping high in the air every ten yards or so. He forded the river and went bounding on, still calling out, towards the village.

Quite calmly I emptied his rifle into the ground, threw all his kit into a bush, and proceeded to net fourteen sea trout.

It was reported to me by my spies the next day that the same keeper had jacked in his job and had arranged to leave the estate even before his notice expired.

CAPERS IN CAITHNESS

ONE MORNING IN the pub I met Jim who informed me, “I’ve just been on my holidays up north, and I’ve never seen so many salmon in all my life.”

At this I nearly choked on my pint. “How long ago?” I asked him.

“Last week. There must have been hundreds of them in a pool no wider than the High Street.”

“When can I go up and have a look?” I enquired, as the local fishing was not so hot.

“Friday,” said Jim. “I’ll use the firm’s shooting brake. We’ll be up there in five hours and back the next day.”

So it was that we made our way to Dornoch, crossing the Bonar Bridge and continuing north to the river Jim had described. It was just on midnight when we got there. Sure enough, the water was teeming with fish. I put on the wet suit, got out the net – and did a daft thing. I left my clothes in the car, and for this I was to pay dearly later on.

Anyhow, I slid into the pool, which was near an old graveyard. It had become very dark. The only sounds were the roar of the lynn and the splashes of the salmon jumping. The dark peaty waters were not at all inviting but we had not come all that way for nothing.

The net was fifteen feet deep and thirty yards long, with a mesh of only two and a half inches. The idea was to catch the fish not by the gills but by the teeth. This method cannot be used in fast running water because the fish get drawn out by the force of the current, but it is excellent in deep silent pools. The net must be stationary, set across the pool at an angle and tethered at each side of the bank. Now collect some big stones, start at the bottom of the pool and drive the fish into the net. They then become entangled by their teeth so that when the net is drawn slowly to the bank they are easy to detach when speed is of the essence.

By the time dawn began to break I had sixty-two bonny fish on the banking – a total weight of nearly ten hundredweight.

"Time to decamp," I said to Jim, who was busy dragging them away in bags to a place near the car, which was parked at three hundred yards distance. So far, so good. The last bag had only four fish in it.

"Get a move on," I said to Jim. "It's getting light."

So off he went with the four fish – and that was the last I saw of him for four days.

As for me, I was dragging two bags of fish from where Jim had dumped them when I heard the car start and saw it shoot off. This indicated that something was wrong, so I dropped the bags and went on cautiously to investigate. Exhausted by the night's work I staggered through the wood to the road, rounded a tree and came face to face with a muckle Highland ghillie.

"What are you doing up here?" he enquired in his quaint drawl. "And dressed like *that*?" He pointed at my wetsuit.

I had to think fast, having hidden the net minutes before – it's still there, incidentally.

"I've been to a fancy dress party in Lairg," I informed him, "and got lost in the heather on my way back to Bonar Bridge."

"Ah well," says he, "I am not one for disbelieving you but I think you should come with me to see the laird or even the police." He then took me by the arm and proceeded to march me to his car. Now, at that point the river runs beside the road and there are a number of smaller pools – deep but not very wide. I made up my mind – it was now or never.

The ghillie was at least a foot bigger than me, and he took bigger strides as well, so I had to play it right. I walked along the road with him until I felt him relaxing his grip on my arm a little. Then, taking a step short I punched him on the kidneys, whereupon he gave a roar and let go. I jumped the fence and made to rush back to the river.

On the other side I turned to see that the punch had had no effect whatever on the ghillie.

“Come back!” he shouted fruitlessly.

“Piss off!” I told him.

“You’ll never get to Ullapool,” he yelled. (Why he said Ullapool, I don’t know) “You’ll never get away from here!”

“That’s all right,” I informed him. “I was in the SAS.”

At this he turned and ran to his car. I could hear it start but could not see it. The village half a mile away had a phone, and I knew it would be anything up to seven minutes before he could contact the laird and the police and whoever else.

I ran to where Jim had left the rest of the fish. (The keeper must have found the bag he had been carrying and thought the four salmon in it were all we had caught.) With not a moment to lose I tipped them into the dried-up gulley, stuffed the bags into a crevice and covered everything up. Within minutes the police arrived in a white van, together with some keepers in a Land Rover and the laird himself in a large car. The laird pointed me out and they all moved towards me at a brisk pace.

The only means of escape was the river itself. I plunged out of sight down the bank, swam to a cleft just above the old graveyard and jammed myself into it. After a time I heard the laird and his men shouting their way along above me. Now I knew how Bonnie Prince Charlie must have felt while being chased by the Redcoats – the only difference here being that these were Bluecoats and I, of course, was no Bonnie Prince!

The keepers moved off upstream, so easing myself out of my watery sanctuary I let the current take me slowly downstream, with my head just showing above water. Keeping close to the side of the river next to the road I swam on and on until I rounded a corner and saw in front of me my biggest obstacle so far. This was a bridge, upon which I observed two policemen, leaning over and watching the water below them.

I pulled myself out and into some ferns. Cut off now from in front and behind, and the right and left, I was faced with something of a dilemma. As I watched, the police turned round and began to look downstream from the far side of the bridge. If I could only get to the bridge and under it before they turned again...

I filled my lungs and made a run for it along the bank. The noise of the stream drowned my pounding footsteps. I reached the bridge and stopped beneath it. After a few minutes there came the sound of shouting from upstream which meant that the keepers were coming back. From the voices directly above me – the officers were talking loudly because of the noise of the river – I judged they had again turned and were giving all their attention to these new sounds. I rushed through the bridge, crawled under a watergate and took to the woods only ten yards away. If they looked over their shoulders they couldn't have failed to see me, but my luck held.

I followed the course of the river until it flowed into the Dornoch Firth. Here there was another problem. The main road ran only a few yards from the shore, with very little cover for anyone on the shore of the firth or in the water. Pulling out my ten-inch knife I hacked some rushes, grass and small branches, tied them with willow bark and placed them on my head.

I then swam slowly down the narrow firth, aware of a police van passing now and again on the nearby road. Eventually I contrived to drift over to the other side, which was wooded and afforded suitable cover. Coming out of the water I began to stagger down a wee glen to where I knew there was a village. Before I reached it I passed close to a little shack with an old man and an equally old dog sitting outside.

As I approached, the old man got up hurriedly and they both went round the back of the house. When I got level, there they were staring at me through the front window! Well, I suppose it was not every day they saw someone in a wet suit staggering down the track, resembling a ballet dancer who has been rolling in a midden!

I reached the village, which is also a railway station, and enquired when the next train was due. It was then one o'clock and the Inverness train was not due until three, so I lay down on a bench for a kip. I had been on the go for more than twenty-four hours and was naturally quite tired.

The train duly arrived and as I had no money I had to spin a yarn about my boat having been sunk in The Minch. For some reason the guard didn't believe me, but he said: "Work it out when you get to Inverness, lad. You can sit in the baggage compartment." They really are very good natured in the far north. So in I went. Unfortunately the luggage van was full of French bicyclists, together with their machines.

I lay down on the floor, dog tired. The Froggies sat and stared at me and my somewhat unusual attire. The biggest one said something to the others and they all burst out laughing. I was in no mood to take any of their nonsense, so I gave them a dirty look, at which I am adept, and informed them, "If you don't stop your gibberish I will ram my fist down your greasy throats."

They never uttered another word until we got to Inverness.

The Edinburgh train was already in and it was no problem to jump on to it. I chose a seat in among a lot of old ladies on an excursion. The one beside me enquired, "Where have you been, son?"

I again related my story of the boat being sunk in The Minch and how I hadn't eaten anything for two days, whereupon she produced a flask of tea and some biscuits, to which I did instant justice. Some of the others also chipped in, so that I was suddenly besieged by pies, buns, cakes, liquorice and throat lozenges.

These agreeable old people were all getting off at Waverley

Station, so naturally I offered to carry as much of their luggage as I could, and thus had no problem getting past the ticket collector. I did, however, receive some funny looks as I crossed Princes Street in my wetsuit on the way to the bus station.

When I got there I immediately met a friend also waiting for the bus to Haddington, and he was kind enough to pay my fare.

It was ten to eleven by the time we arrived and so, choking for a pint, I entered the bar nearest the bus stop. Because I was known there I easily obtained a drink on tick. Just as I was downing the last of it and contemplating another, the local police sergeant and a constable discreetly walked in.

"Can I have a word with you outside?" says the sarge. So of course I had no option but to go.

"Were you up in the Highlands recently?" he enquires.

"I'm not sure where it was," I said.

"How come the fancy dress?" He pointed at my wetsuit.

"I've been at a party," I said truthfully.

"I think you'd better attend at the station," says the sarge. I was duly frog-marched to the nick.

It was there that I found out what had happened to Jim. He had been walking up to the car when the ghillie saw him. Jim dropped the fish and drove off. He stopped at the village phone box to make a call, goodness knows why. The ghillie arrived and removed the keys from Jim's car. Jim then spilled all the beans. I now stood charged with poaching four salmon.

"What do you want to do?" asked the sergeant. "Admit it and you'll get off lightly, but you'll have to make your own way back up there. If not, we'll lock you up now and take you up ourselves."

Not particularly anxious to spend a weekend in the nick, I told them I had indeed removed four fish from that Highland river. So off home I went to tell the family all about it. Having done that, I went round to Jim's house and told his wife, who promptly went into hysterics.

I was to report to the Highland police station at ten o'clock on Monday morning. On Sunday evening I collected Jim's other car and with his wife and bairns as passengers set off again for the far north, sightseeing on the way.

At nine o'clock, just after dark, we were once again beside the same river, parked in a lay-by not far from where I had hidden the other fifty-eight salmon in the dried-up burn. I cautiously approached the place and found them as I had left them. It took nearly an hour to drag them to the vicinity of the car.

As I was doing this, my wife was asleep in the driving seat in case anyone came along – and that's just what happened. The very same ghillie drove up and shone his torch at her and the bairns. Telling them they were not allowed to stay the night there, he went off, satisfied they were tourists. I lay hidden in the heather ten yards away.

I gave him fifteen minutes and then loaded the fish into the back of the car, covered them with a blanket and sat the bairns on top. Ten miles from the small town we stopped and tried to sleep. Just before dawn my wife woke me up, whispering, "There's something screeching in the heather over there." Sure enough, a hideous wailing came from the moorland close at hand.

"It's only a wildcat," I assured her. "It's probably smelt the fish."

We tried to sleep again, but the howling of the beast made it impossible. I picked up a stone and threw it, and the cat bounded away for fifty yards and proceeded to make more noise than ever.

I reported to the police station, where the sergeant informed me that the case had been put back until eleven o'clock. His constable then kindly took us all on a tour of the village.

The sheriff fined Jim £100. I got £20. Jim got his shooting brake back and I reclaimed my clothes. Jim shot off saying, "I'll meet you in Haddington."

As Fate would have it, our car needed a shove to start it. The police obliged. By this time the fish had begun to smell, and with the police noses only a few inches away it was unbelievable that they never caught a whiff. We then gave them a big wave and they waved back.

We sold the fish in Edinburgh.

When I met Jim next time he said, "Where's my cut?"

I handed him £10. "That's your lot," I informed him. "It's for the hire of your car!"

THE CHINESE SYNDICATE

I HAVE A SPECIAL liking for Chinese food and that is what took me to The Orchid – a take-away establishment offering Chinese dishes and other Eastern fare.

In the course of time I got to know Harry, the Hong Kong Chinese cook, pretty well, and one day he asked me if I could obtain any rabbits for him.

I asked him how many and he said half a dozen would be acceptable. The next day I presented six rabbits, for which he paid me not in money but in curried King prawns and similar delicacies.

Rabbits then became a regular order and a few weeks later my Chinese friend said to me, "Ted, I have my bosses coming from Hong Kong and I tell them about your labbits" – he could not say rabbits properly – "and they would like very much to shoot some."

"Is there not," I enquired politely, "plenty of labbits in Hong Kong?"

"Not wild ones," he replied.

I happened to have my oldest son Andrew with me at the time and he, being a bit of a joker, says to Chinese Harry: "Of course you know that at this time of year labbits live up tlees."

I didn't like to say anything in front of the man myself, in case he thought we were sending him up, so later I said to Andrew, "We'll need to think of something, for maybe there's £100 in this for us – and a bit of a laugh too. Get the rest of the lads and go and ferret some rabbits for next Saturday – that'll be the day of the shoot."

Harry was then asked to inform his bosses that they should be outside the local hotel at midday, where I would be waiting to take them to the estate. (Previously I had told them how I had the use of a lot of ground for shooting and fishing – omitting to mention that visits were only possible after dark, when all the keepers and bailiffs were in bed.)

On Saturday morning we selected a section of the forest that was mostly hardwood. Being December, there was very little foliage about.

The rabbits we had earlier killed we had jammed among the branches about six feet off the ground within a radius of about a hundred yards down each side of the ride, where they would not be difficult for the visiting sportsmen to see and shoot.

It was a hard job getting the Chinamen organised as they spoke very little English. Take-away Harry had, of course, explained to them how the local labbits hid up tlees in winter, and when this was repeated back to us we had a bit of difficulty keeping a straight face. Anyway, off we set – five of us and five of them.

With me was a Chinese with a lovely shotgun. He acted as interpreter. As we moved forward in line – in case our guests got excited and shot someone – I suddenly seized the interpreter by the arm and pointed out a rabbit apparently peering at him from the branches of a beech tree.

He responded by putting in three rapid shots, blowing it to pieces. My lads then followed suit, pointing out the game and then rushing forward to give the corpse a quick shake, as though it was in its death throes, before stuffing it into their bags.

This went on for nearly an hour, until I called a halt and said to my lads, "The keepers will have had their dinner by now and will be on the move. When I give the signal, tell the Chinks we must go back to the wagon to collect more ammo for the guns."

Sure enough, ten minutes later we observed the yellow-topped Land Rover making its way up the farm road towards us.

"Right lads," I ordered. "Move back to the van and call in our friends."

What happened next I found out from the police in Dunbar later that night.

When the keepers encountered the five Chinese, we were nowhere to be seen, of course. The somewhat bewildered sportsmen were asked who had given them permission to shoot. Harry stated that he thought anybody could shoot labbits once they had taken to the tlees, and pointed out one which had not yet been blasted out of the branches.

The keepers duly escorted them to the police station, where they repeated their story to the inspector and, of course, gave him a description of ourselves. Upon hearing the whole story the police went into hysterical laughter, gave them back their guns and warned them to be more particular in future about who they chose to host their shooting parties.

As for us, we never got paid for laying on the afternoon's sport – but we had many a laugh at home and in the pub for a good few weeks to come.

NEARLY KILLED!

I WAS DOWN BY the river as usual one day in the autumn, on the look-out for salmon or sea trout. As I peered over the bank into the water I saw, about three feet down, the tail of a fish. From where I was I had no chance of putting a snare over him, so I crawled a little way downstream, slipped into the water and proceeded to snare him from there.

He turned out to be a nice seven pound sea trout, but as it thrashed about and I was preparing to throw it on the bank I heard a sudden roar. Turning round I beheld the head keeper on the opposite bank emerging from a patch of wild rhubarb.

"Leave ma fish alane, ye poaching bastard!" he fairly screamed at me.

"Get lost, ye daft auld bugger," I responded.

At this he seemed to lose the head entirely and rushed off out of sight, probably heading for his Land Rover.

I got the fish out of the water, killed him and stuffed him into my pocket. I was bolting back the way I had come when, from behind me, a shot rang out. I could hardly believe it when what was certainly a rifle bullet struck the ground a few yards to my left.

Bent double, I ran on, climbed a dyke and plunged into a tattie field where I covered myself with shaws. From there I was able to watch the keeper, who was carrying both a rifle and a shotgun, storming down the river bank followed by the under-keeper.

"I'll kill the bastard for this!" I heard him say, in a voice that was gibbering with rage.

He suddenly put down the shotgun and began to blaze away with his .22 rifle, aiming at anything around him in his madness. He couldn't see where I was, but one bullet actually caused the small blue flowers of the tattie plant to cascade onto my head, and another hit a stone not six inches away, so that tiny fragments of lead actually stuck in my face. I was becoming somewhat alarmed when suddenly the firing ceased. Holding a bunch of tattie shaws as camouflage I gingerly looked up to see the under-keeper struggling to restrain his superior.

"Stop it, Willie!" I heard him protest. "You'll kill him!"

"He's not going to steal ma fish," gurgled the old keeper, who had completely flipped his lid and was slavering like a rabid dog.

I crawled off along the drill, reached the hedge and made my escape.

I then did something I had never done before: I complained to the police. I showed them the marks on my face, which I still have to this day.

"Ah well," the police said. "It's your own fault, Ted. You shouldn't go annoying him like that, should you?"

So much for justice!

THE BRAES OF MAR

"TED," SAID TAM as we were having a pint in the pub one morning in November, "did you see in the papers about the red deer near Blair Atholl? They're so tame from hunger they'll eat out of your hand."

"Say no more," says I. "Do you fancy a run up anywhere north and see if we can nick a couple? Some of them weigh twenty stones, and that's a lot of cash. I've got some old single ball cartridges from the Second War and they still work and should bring down a stag, no bother."

So it was that we all set forth in Tam's thirty hundredweight van. He had with him a .22 rifle and a double 12-bore. I had a single 12-bore. Willy and Jim came along as well.

The weather was very bad. There was heavy snow in the Highlands, with more to come. We reached Perth about two o'clock, stopped for a bite to eat, then pushed on again till we came to the Devil's Elbow, which was very tricky to negotiate.

A mile outside Braemar we saw our first red deer, standing quite close to the road. At the time, Tam was the only one of us who could legally drive, so I said to Jim, "Bring the double 12-bore and I'll take the single."

Tam dropped us off, intending to go up the road to the village and turn the van. This would give us ample time to obtain one or two hinds.

By this time it was fairly dark, but the deer could easily be seen against the snow. I stalked a big old hind standing near a pile of turnips. I got within thirty-five yards and fired, and she went down. The sound of the shot echoed for miles into the hills. Someone would no doubt be along soon to investigate.

Jim came up, panting like a horse.

"Get hold of the back leg," I told him, "and let's get out of here." We duly dragged the beast to the side of the road.

There we waited for what seemed like a long time, but in fact after only ten minutes Tam appeared with the truck and we all lent a hand to lift the deer into the back. A car approached, so we all gathered round the back wheel as though we had a puncture.

"Quick," said Tam. "Let's get the Hell out of here." He was very agitated and indeed had a tale to tell himself.

Seemingly as he got in to Braemar he was alarmed to see, lit up by the headlights, a local policeman standing at a garden gate with a cup of tea in his hand. Somewhat abashed, Tam drove straight on, turned, and came back. The bobby was still there.

As we all drove southwards down the road, we got this garbled story from Tam, but did not think to ditch the deer or the equipment. We drove for some time, through Angus, into Perthshire and began to think we would get away with it. Not at all. We rounded a z-bend and there was a police road block. As it was on a hill and very icy, we could not back off. Next thing, there was a constable peering in at the window.

"Well, lads," says he. "What are yea up to?"

"We've been skiing," I informed him.

"Oh aye. Where's your skiing gear, then?" he asked, as well he might, considering our appearance.

"We hired it," I said.

"You don't look like skiers to me." This was fair enough as we were all wearing boiler suits and wellingtons.

"Get out," he says. I got out.

His mate, a sergeant, was opening the back door, and immediately his torch flashed onto the body of the big hind.

"Poachers!" he yells. The constable grabbed me and tried to put on the danglers (handcuffs). Naturally, I attempted to avoid this.

Thinking that his colleague was being attacked, the constable drew his truncheon and smacked Willy on the nose shouting, "There's another five of us up the road!"

During this melee I took the opportunity to jump over the wall and run for it. After about thirty yards my wellingtons became full of snow and slush, so that all I could do was walk. The sergeant was on me in no time. I slumped down and went limp as he put the handcuffs on – because if you do that it takes a lot to lift you.

"I've caught you this time, my lad," says he.

"I'm not able to walk," I informed him. "I've got a bad heart and haven't been taking the tablets all this week."

By causing this diversion I hoped to give the others time to make good their escape, but the daft idiots just sat there and did nothing. (Tam was anyway suffering from shock, or alcohol, or both, and a sore nose.)

As if by magic there now appeared a Black Maria, and we were all put in it.

Poor Willy was still clutching his bloody neb. He tried to speak, but all he got was, "Save it for the Sheriff the morn."

We were then taken to Perth Police Station and duly locked up. Ironically for me the Station stands on the site of what was the Queen's Barracks, once the depot of my old regiment, The Black Watch. I had enlisted there sixteen years before and spent many a weekend in army detention in the jail.

Next morning we were taken to the cells below the Sheriff Courthouse and waited our turn to be tried.

"Bring up the poachers!" called the court sergeant, and we all emerged to meet our worst adversary yet in the form of a Sheriff who was a ruthless detester of poachers and sheep-stealers and the like.

Our lawyer was a pessimist if ever there was one. "You'll all get time!" he told us gleefully.

As we lined up to be tried, Willy was called out first.

The Sheriff looked at his record sheet.

"He's not done anything like this before," said the lawyer.

"Perhaps not," said the Sheriff, "but he seems to have done just about everything else."

He gave Willy a look of disdain and went on studying the rest of the crime sheets. We hung our heads and said nothing, as it was clear he had the upper hand.

"So," says the Sheriff at last. "You people think you can come up here and plunder the countryside with impunity, do you? It's a heinous and serious crime you've committed," he informed us, and we all stood there expecting to be given three months each.

Instead, he said: "I fine you each £125, and your equipment is confiscated."

We then found ourselves on the road to Edinburgh, which was forty miles away.

Being a somewhat disagreeable set of cops, they also confiscated our wellingtons, so that we cursed them and the miserable old Sheriff every mile as we trudged down the icy road in our socks. Eventually, however, a lorry driver stopped, and as he was going down the A1 he put us off within a mile of our homes. Meanwhile our feet thawed out and we found that the forced march had not done us any great harm.

We arrived back in Haddington to a somewhat mixed reception. In the pub, at least, there was a round of applause. Word of our deeds had gone before us in the form of television and radio news. Tam was terrified to inform his wife of his return, but after eight pints of lager he managed to raise enough courage. We heard the next morning that he had to suffer the worst tongue-lashing of his life, but because he looked so pathetic standing there in his frayed and battered socks, she was content to leave it at that!

THE BEAST IN THE LOCH

"I'M THINKING ABOUT a lynn up north which is fairly full of Red Fellows," I said one day to my mate Jock. (Red Fellows are salmon. In fishermen's parlance the word salmon is unlucky, and there is a long list of other words used to signify the fish.) "If you fancy a run up, using your wagon, we'll go fifty-fifty on the catch."

I had in fact been up the week before and earned £750 for four hours' fishing.

"Okay," says Jock, envisaging a few easy quid.

"We'll go on Friday, arrive at dark and net the lynns. We can be away before daybreak."

We decided to go there by a different route this time in case we were being watched by the police, who had been given my description at Inverness after a previous expedition. So off we went, stopping at Callander for a few pints, which made us late, so that when we finally came to a loch we stopped for a tin of stout and a rest.

After about fifteen minutes I noticed that a large number of lovely grilse were leaping out of the water not twenty-five yards from the bank.

"Quick Jock," I says. "Get the kit out of the boot. We'll try a fling of the net here. These are lovely fish and they may save us a lot of time."

By this time it was 2.45am and the early summer dawn comes quickly in the Highlands, so I climbed into the wetsuit and took the other end of the net.

"Hold the other end," I told Jock, "and I'll swim out."

This was a strangle net, one hundred and ten metres long and thirty meshes deep, made of very strong nylon and able to hold a forty pound salmon without difficulty.

Holding the end of the net in my teeth I proceeded to swim

out into the loch. I had not gone far when I felt the tugging and jerking as the first fish hit. When the net became taut I stood up in the water and waited as the fish went on colliding with it at a good rate.

Suddenly I felt a strong, irresistible pressure on my right leg and felt the net being drawn as if by great force further up the loch. I managed to keep hold of it, but there was nothing I could do. Something was dragging and tearing through the net in a way I had never known before.

I yelled to Jock to haul me in but he couldn't, and now my left hand was caught in the mesh and I was being pulled along by whatever it was. Then came a great swirl in the water. I was aware of something massive rising from the depths and, for a few seconds, felt a skin with the texture of a piece of emery paper or the bark of a beech tree. I then wrenched my hand away and swam in a panic for the shore, where I bolted up the bank. Jock and I looked at each other flabbergasted.

We sat in the car till about seven o'clock and then ventured down to see what had happened to the net and the fish.

We found the net and started to pull it in, ready to run like hell if the thing we had caught should appear again. I thought it might have been a seal, but Jock reckoned it was something very much bigger. When we finally retrieved the net we found a hole you could have driven a bus through. Whatever had hit it had done so with great force, totally ruining it.

There were, however, still twelve salmon of about nine pounds each entangled in the rest of it, so we were not too badly off.

To end the story, Jock reported our adventure to the editor of the local paper, who duly published it. I am left with the thought that whatever came close to me in the dark water of that loch was certainly no seal. I am sure of that, as I have met up with seals many times in the Tyne estuary at Dunbar, and the holes they make are a mere five feet in circumference. Neither did they behave like a shark or porpoise.

If none of these, what was it..?

THE GAME COCK

I MET ANDREW in the pub one day and, over a pint, I said to him: "I hear you're a breeder of fighting cocks. I'm looking for one to use its feathers to make flies for the fishing." I was telling a lie, for I had very different plans, as you will hear.

So I gave him ten shillings (as the money was then) and got myself a young cock. I kept and fed it for four months, by which time it was fully grown and crowing like a demented bullfrog.

A month earlier I had seen the keepers on the estate releasing their hand-reared pheasants, so the birds would now be big enough to kill. I had made a pair of spurs for the fighting cock, which had put on full plumage and was attempting to murder anything it saw.

It was now December. I got up before dawn, took the bird and made my way to where I had seen the largest gathering of pheasants. The gentry were about due to have their big shoot, so the pheasants had not much longer to live. At a place where the keepers had dumped some grain I put on the spurs. These were, in fact, old darts sharpened to needle points and facing inwards.

I staked him out in a clearing on thirty yards of twine, took the old sock off his head and left him to it. Sure enough, he began to crow as though announcing the end of the world. I concealed myself in a hedge to watch the outcome.

As dawn began to break, the pheasants roosting in the spruce wood nearby began to flutter down, attracted by the calls of the intruder.

Fifteen minutes went by and still the fighting cock crowed. Then, suddenly, advancing to do battle, came the first victim. This was an old cock pheasant, a veteran of many wars and, by his manner, the champion of the seven-acre wood. (For a hand-reared pheasant, five seasons is a long time to live.)

Now he advanced on the gamecock, throwing out his chest and hopping from side to side like a boxer. Finally he made a sudden rush with his hackles up. What happened next took only a few seconds. The gamecock jumped into the air and brought its spurs together on each side of the pheasant's head, killing him instantly.

I broke cover and retrieved the corpse. That morning we obtained five cock pheasants (fairly quietly, no gunshots!) all in the same way.

AN EPISODE ON GALA WATER

"I HEAR THE BOYS over by Gala are getting a good kill of fish these days," I said to my mate, Jock. "It's time we took a wee birl down there. How about tomorrow night?"

"Aye, fine," replies he, as he always does. It was the middle of November, with the sky full of stars, frost on the ground – good weather for salmon.

So off we set in an old and unroadworthy car of the kind the police immediately confiscate. It took us only half an hour to get to the place and change into our wetsuits.

Carrying the splash net, pick shafts, tattie bags and hoods for over our heads, we made our way down the old railway line and over a drystane dyke. Halfway across the field we became aware of some cows, and even more so of a very big white bull. This animal gazed at us carefully but took no action. More of this later.

We hid the bags and got the net stretched across the burn and proceeded, at a slow pace, to plunder the water in our accustomed manner. After ten minutes we hit fish and soon had bagged seven good-sized salmon.

All of a sudden I saw a light approaching and whispered to Jock: "Let's bugger off at great speed!"

"Aye, fine that," said Jock.

Just then the bailiffs' dogs caught our scent and the fun really started.

"Get after the bastards!" roared a voice.

Grabbing the net and fish we departed rapidly the way we had come, with what sounded like all the Braw Lads of Gala Water hot on our heels.

Halfway across the same field we paused to listen, but the chase seemed to have changed direction. We continued at a more leisurely pace.

Clouds had come over, so that we almost bumped into the cows before we saw them, and they began to mill about. So did the big white bull. This time he didn't stop at merely watching us. He let out a bellow of rage and came straight for us from a distance of about thirty yards.

Naturally we took to our heels, but it is not easy to avoid a charging bull while carrying a net, pick shafts and a bagful of salmon. However, I broke into a gallop myself – all in vain. Before I could climb the dyke he caught up with me and tossed me over it into a sea of mud.

After several minutes I collected myself, gingerly retrieved the fish from the other side of the wall (the victorious bull had walked away) and staggered off in the direction of the hotel where we had agreed to meet. There I found Jock had preceded me, and as I came into the bar somewhat muddy and nursing a cracked rib, the locals all roared and laughed.

"Everyone kens a' aboot yon bull," an old worthy told us gleefully. "The bailiffs have had a lot of trouble with him. They'd sooner jump in the river than cross that field after ye!"

A CLOSE RUN THING

AS USUAL, WE HAD made pigs of ourselves at Christmas, having eaten and drunk everything we could lay our hands on.

"There's nothing for the New Year's dinner," quoth the wife.

"Dinnae worry, hen," I assured her. "I'll try and rustle something up."

Rustle was the correct word, for as soon as it was dark I and a mate slipped out of the house and made our way to The Provider's estate. (We called him The Provider because his very large piece of land provided us with just about everything we needed in the way of food!)

We soon came upon some white-faced Cheviot sheep feeding in a patch of turnips, obviously being fattened up for the table. It was a simple operation to drive the young ewes into a corner of the field, then perform a mad run and throw ourselves in among them, grab one by the wool and swiftly despatch it. It took but a few more seconds to carry it to the burn, suspend it from a tree and partly butcher it. After skinning and gutting we took it nearer to the house and left it to hang, well-hidden in a thicket.

The next worry was how to get the dinner actually into the house on the other side of town without arousing suspicion. I had an idea. Getting out the family pram, I commandeered it (after a bit of harassment from the bairn) and with the wife wheeled it to the scene of the crime.

The beast still had its head on. Having wrapped it in a sheet we put an old bonnet of the bairn's on it. I then instructed the wife to push the vehicle through the town as if we were out for a walk with the child.

Unfortunately, as we strolled casually along the main street, we bumped into an old friend who was somewhat the worse for drink.

"And how's the bairn the day?" he enquired.

To my horror, before I could stop him he had lifted the covers back to peer at the passenger in the pram.

"Goad, he's awfu' pale-looking," he exclaimed, drawing back a pace. "And there's something wrong with its lug!"

"Aye, right enough, we're just off to the doctor," I informed him, hastily covering the face and, at the same time, observing a member of the local constabulary walking towards us. Crossing to the other side of the street we left old Willie gazing after us in a worried manner, but we arrived home without more ado.

We dumped the body into the bath and got busy on the rest of the work, as this was now Hogmany. Suddenly the bairn appeared and asked what was in the bath.

"It's a monkey," I told her, for want of a better word, and off she went to play with her pals.

Now it happened that at that time I had in the cellar a kestrel with a damaged wing. I had managed to pin the joint, but the bird still needed a rest before I could let it go. I was keeping it in the dark until it recovered. I was in the act of feeding it when I heard a lot of giggling from upstairs and found half a dozen of the bairn's pals gazing in awe at the 'monkey' in the bath. I let out a roar and they all bolted.

I duly finished dismembering the beast and early next morning delivered the joints to the wife to put in the oven while I went first footing.

I came back five hours later, gibbering drunk, with a few of my mates. The wife had been slaving away cooking *all* the mutton. This, as it turned out, was just as well.

We were coming to the end of what had been a really tasty New Year's dinner when I heard the well-known screech of tyres outside.

"Quick!" I shouted. "Lock the doors! Pull the curtains! We've got fifteen minutes to eat the last of this meat!"

As the hammering on the doors began – back and front – we all started to gorge ourselves anew. We ate like mad things – my our jaws were going like hamster's.

"Come on, Ted, open up!" shouted the sergeant. "We ken whit ye've been up to!"

One of the bairns must have talked. Never mind. We ignored this untimely disturbance and continued to cram mutton down our throats. After ten minutes they knocked the front door in, but by that time the only incriminating evidence was several bones, one being chewed by the bairn, another by the lurcher.

"We have reason to believe," said the sergeant, "that you are in possession of stolen meat on these premises – in the form of one Cheviot sheep."

I mumbled words to the effect that I knew nothing about any such thing – I was unable to speak properly as my mouth was full of exactly what he was talking about.

They searched the house but, of course, found nothing and duly congregated again in the living room.

"Where is it, then?" demanded a young cop.

"Ah dinnae ken whit you're on aboot," I told him, dislodging the last of the mutton from between my teeth.

The sergeant reappeared.

"What's the bird doing in your coal cellar?" he enquired.

"Oh, that's a tufted owl," I told him.

"Doesnae look like an owl to me," he says suspiciously.

"Oh it's verra rare," I assured him, trying my best to keep my face straight. "It roosts in there by day and catches mice at night."

Attention now turned to the young cop, who was attempting to take the bone away from the bairn in order to inspect it more closely, but the bairn was resisting with some considerable noise.

Observing this, the wife rushed over and struck the constable on the arm with an alloy pot.

"Whit? Steal the bairn's dinner, wud ye?" she yelled in a voice loud enough to be overheard by most of the neighbours in the street.

Taken aback, and having found no conclusive evidence, and no doubt because they had their own New Year dinners to go to, the sergeant and his men gave up and departed the festive scene, leaving me to repair the lock and hinges of my oft-broken door!

GLOSSARY

Polis	(police)
Cockinny	(Cockenzie, an East Lothian fishing village)
Hornies	(police)
Jyle	(jail)
Jam	(know)
Grunie	(bag)
Gadgie	(man)
Nash off	(leave quickly)
Chored them for the pannie	(stole them for the pot)
Tober oot	(rush away)
Stadie's deekin at us	(the cops are watching us)